CHOOSE *Life*

A Midwest Mom's Life Miracles

Carol J. Nelson

Choose Life: A Midwest Mom's Life Miracles

ISBN 979-8-88751-134-4 (paperback)
ISBN 979-8-88751-135-1 (digital)

Christian Faith Publishing
832 Park Avenue
Meadville, PA 16335
www.christianfaithpublishing.com

Printed in the United States of America

INTRODUCTION

I do not want the focus of this book to be about me or how special our family was or is; I want anyone reading this book to know I am just an ordinary person in an everyday world with an opportunity and responsibility to "choose" how I respond to the situations that life brings my way. This is a story about how God can intervene in any circumstance involving any ordinary person if they choose to let Him. "See, I set before you today life and prosperity, death and destruction" (Deuteronomy 30:15 NIV).

I am not special, and God is not partial to anyone but responds to *all* who diligently seek Him and often to those who do not. He does not care how many bad habits we have or how selfish, self-centered, jealous, angry, bitter, or hateful we are. He meets us right where we are. Believe me, I have been all those things and still grapple with those tendencies all the time. In fact, He delights in using the worst of us, redeeming us day by day, patiently and gently, to be more like Him.

Prologue

This is an account, a true story, of a *few* of God's interventions into the very ordinary, normal, everyday life of a housewife and mother of five wonderful children in the '70s and '80s. It also includes a few instances of his intervention in the lives of my husband and myself where it may bring some clarity.

This was an era when women were seeking emancipation from the traditional roles of wife and mother and were going after goals of self-realization and fulfillment and equality with men (in the areas of career and equal pay).

After deep consideration of all these opportunities, guess what I chose? To be married with children, and not just one or two, but as time went on, five! This was, of course, politically incorrect, but it was what I wanted. Yes, I expected my choice would be more of a mundane, perhaps monotonous, and mediocre existence.

Boy! Was I wrong!

Any life path has moments of dull routine, but if we never experienced the occasional depths of depression, we would never be able to experience the exhilaration of real joy when it comes. Or, perhaps, we find out that what we thought would make us happy, when we achieve it, is only temporary, empty, and maybe not as fulfilling as we thought. Well, I have lived a full life now, and I have never regretted my choice. Here are just *some* of the moments that made it so precious.

CHAPTER 1

My Worst Nightmare

It is mid-October 1977. The leaves quickly change and fall in central Minnesota, and on this cloudy October morning, most of the leaves had already left the trees. I remember just a couple of weeks earlier, we were rushing down this same Park Avenue, four-lane, one-way early on a bright, clear sky morning, brilliant leaves on both sides, anticipating the arrival of our second born with excitement and some trepidation. He was two weeks early, not to be born on his due date like his big brother!

This time we are heading to the same hospital emergency room with our two-week-old son with a 104-degree fever. During the last few hours, he had developed this terrifying fever with convulsive head movements. Immediately, they explain to us that these symptoms warrant a spinal tap. My mind flashes back to watching such a procedure in nurses' training, but it was on an adult, not a tiny two-week-old infant! I cringe at the thought, and they quickly usher us out of the room as they carry in the six-inch-long needle on a tray to be injected into his tiny spine to remove spinal fluid and check for serious disease.

I do not remember ever being so frightened in all my twenty-five years. His cries of pain, never heard by this mother in all of his short life, are still ringing in my ears thirty minutes later as a doctor returns and closes the door ominously. He explains, quite matter-of-factly, that the test revealed a diagnosis of meningitis. More tests will reveal whether it is viral or bacterial. If it is bacterial, it should respond to the penicillin administered to him immediately. Viral meningitis has no known treatment at present. In either case, our son would remain in the hospital for at least ten days with these three prospects:

1.   Possible mental retardation
2.   Possible physical handicaps
3.   Possible death

He was obviously preparing us for the worst, especially in a child so young, but we were speechless and heartbroken. Mom was on the way from the Chicago area to be with us. They told me I would not be able to stay in the hospital with him because of my complications at birth, that I was unable to breast feed, and that he would be fed intravenously. The best we could do for him was to go home and wait. With the heaviest of hearts, we returned home to our eldest son and an empty bassinet.

Loneliness, emptiness, isolation, and silence (and these words are inadequate to express the sorrow) totally enveloped us that first night. The uninterrupted hours of our newborn not waking us for his three-hour feeding were full of torture and unrest. I went through every detail of that day in my mind over and over, tormenting myself with what I could have done differently. Going back over the events, a quiet voice reminded me of one event, twenty minutes on the way to the hospital, that stands out in my mind.

Yesterday morning, after a restless night, little Ben developed a fever that started at 101 degrees and quickly rose to 104 by early afternoon. We debated whether we should go into the emergency room but decided to call when the fever spiked and cool baths and clothes were not bringing it down. They encouraged us to come right in, and they would be waiting for him. As we raced down that one-way street on that dreary afternoon, I found myself pleading with God to not let my son die!

His birth had been two weeks early, with many complications and unexpected financial costs, as well as both of us having to stay in the hospital for an extended time. So we were having our first peaceful week at home; our new family of four was just getting acquainted and adjusting when *this* happened!

"God," I argued, "we went through so much to have this little one and now, at two weeks, are You going to take him from us?"

So went the pleas and arguments all the way to the hospital until, finally, I felt myself surrendering. I was reminded of the story of Abraham, of whom God asked, and he became willing to sacrifice his own promised son, miraculously born to his ninety-year-old wife Sarah. This had always been an incomprehensible story of obedience that turned out *good*.

"Father, is this how You felt about giving up Your only Son, Jesus?"

I actually had never had a conversation like this, although I believed in God, but this was a desperate situation.

"If You want our son back so soon, I will give him back to You, Lord."

I heard a whisper in my heart, *Would you still love me if I took Benjamin now?*

I am remembering all I went through at his birth: the cord wrapped around his neck; the huge blood clot in my womb, passing like a second child; the bowel obstruction and extreme pain as my intestines were untangled; and especially not being able to nurse him, which could have been a comfort and healing for both of us after all this trauma.

As it turned out, he was the smallest of our five children and the only one that came early. When he was placed tenderly in my arms, looking as contented as could be, after struggling for that first breath with the cord wrapped around his neck, I realized what a miracle I held in my arms. He looked so much like a teddy bear that I wanted to name him Teddy, but we settled on Benjamin John, such a fighter to be born early too!

"We went through all of this, Lord, and you still want him back?" No answer.

"Alright, your will be done, and yes, I will still love you."

Well, Mom arrived the next day, and then a strange thing happened. An elder from our community church knocked on the door. He told us our son had been put on a prayer chain line and, literally, thousands of people were praying for him (this was 1977, before social media or cell phones). The man looked at Wayne and said, "Benjamin is going to be okay."

"Uh, thanks for all the prayers," Wayne replied, looking down.

"No, Wayne, Ben is going to be fine," he said, looking directly into his eyes. At this point, Wayne began to believe the elder's words.

Some mothers called me that day saying they had been praying prostrate on the floor, interceding.

As soon as we could, we were back at the hospital where our son was strapped flat on his back on a board, spread eagle style with his arms and legs, being intravenously fed, and unable to move. His tiny body looked so miserable, and the sound of my voice through the glass hardly made a difference. Again, just holding and cuddling him was not allowed. Ten days of this! I didn't know if I could stand it, although I knew of other mothers and situations where they had no choice and did get through it.

We watched and waited all day, hardly eating; Mom was at home cooking for us. I think she could not bear to come, so she was trying her best to be helpful. When visiting hours were over, we returned again to an empty bassinet (which I vowed to burn if this turned out badly), and I began to envision the dreadful sight of a tiny casket.

As the evening progressed, Wayne and Mom were quiet and somehow, I was beginning to feel peace and calm. Maybe resignation, as I did sleep that night, remembering my promise to the Lord to love Him no matter the outcome. If this was His doing, He would carry me through it.

As we awoke the next morning, everyone was sober when we received an early morning phone call. Ben's temperature was dropping, and he seemed to be responding. We were encouraged not to be too hopeful because the bad news was that it was not due to the penicillin. They could not get a culture, so it was viral and not bacterial, for which there was no treatment. Yet they were surprised by his quick turnaround on the third day. The nurse said he would still need to be observed for ten days, but the doctor would be in soon to check on him.

Shortly, we received a call from his doctor, who said that *everything* had checked out normal. He sounded very surprised and encouraged and said, "You might as well take him home. He will do much better there than here, but we will need to check him weekly for a month, and then monthly to rule out mental or physical abnormalities." He did not want to get our hopes up too high, but we could tell he was quite puzzled by the case (originally projecting ten days, at the least; again, this was only three days later).

Well, we went back for all his checkups and tests, and all were normal. In fact, he grew up to be a healthy, smart, and tough little boy with a kind and gentle spirit, a pitcher on the baseball team, a love for swimming and skateboarding, and went to Michigan State University and got a degree in business, and is still a Spartans fan to this day.

We were elated, as you can imagine. Even the doctors scratched their heads and said it was amazing and it was nothing they did. This was better than our wildest dreams of maybe months or years of anguish, even if he did survive. In the back of our minds, we thought all of our work together in a Crippled Children's Home in North Dakota, where Wayne and I met in college, could have been preparation for a disabled child.

How did this change your life, you may ask? Well, for the first time, I had no doubt that God can heal and do miracles. For years, I had heard of such things, some even from an acquaintance or friend, but somehow, I doubted whether it could happen to me. This was a turning point, and my son and I have a special relationship where we know there is a purpose for us on this earth. I will never again doubt whether God *can* do miracles; Ben is one. This is not to say He always will. He is always sovereign and has His reasons for everything that we may not understand at the time, but we can reason with Him and have a relationship with Him, which is a discovery that really changed my whole life and perception. There are many similar things I have experienced with each of my children throughout my whole life, and my knowledge of Him is constantly growing and changing, but this is where it all began.

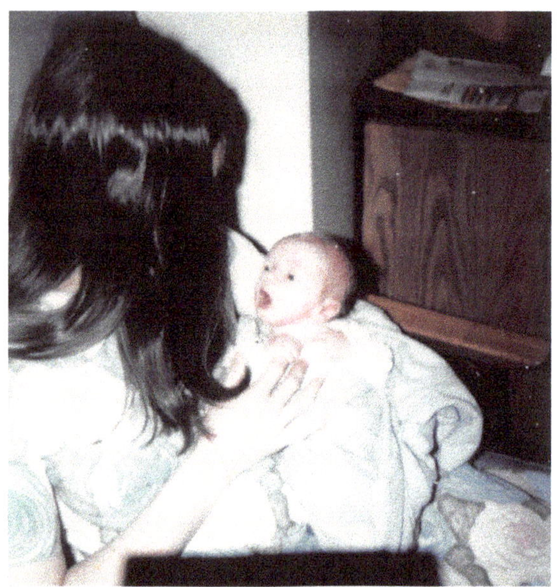

Nate at birth

Two Little Boys in Fifteen Months

Living in a big city with heavy traffic and two small children presents a challenge, and it was no different for us. We had moved from a moderate town, Grand Forks, North Dakota, to the large metropolis of Minneapolis, Minnesota. Both of us had always lived in small towns or suburbs growing up, so Minneapolis was the first large metropolitan city for each of us. Add to that the fact that I was a young, inexperienced mother with two small children only fifteen months apart and living hundreds of miles from either set of grandparents, and you will have to admit that this was an especially big challenge for the two of us. However, I do not believe that we at all realized, at that time, how difficult it would prove to be! We were young and courageous and could accomplish anything.

We lived in a two-bedroom apartment in a brick four-plex on the busy street of Nicollet Avenue, right in the downtown area. At that time, our boys, Nathaniel and

Benjamin, were four and two. We had two close calls to wake us up to the realities of city life and parenthood happening at the same time.

Nate, the older, and Ben, the younger, have personalities as different as night and day. Nate was alert at two days old and processing everything around him. As we carried him out of the hospital, his eyes followed the ceiling lights, one after the other, as we walked down the hallway. Ben slept a lot and seemed content most of the time, while his brother was awake and wanting attention most of the time, taking tiny ten-minute catnaps after feedings. Nate continued to be super observant and quick to learn as we would soon find out.

Ben was relaxed and fun-loving, a happy, trusting baby who took two good naps a day. I do not remember Nate ever taking more than a ten-minute nap up until his brother was born. So you can imagine my apprehension at having two babies; I was not going to have any time to myself, especially with Wayne working long hours and trying to establish himself with a new painting business! Yet lo and behold, after Ben was born, Nate fell asleep in the afternoon at the same time Ben took his second nap (so I actually had more time to myself after Ben was born). God knows all things, doesn't He? And He never gives us more than we can handle, if we listen to Him and trust Him.

Nathaniel was really showing some responsibility and oversight for his little brother. Earlier in the year, he had almost started the stove and kitchen on fire when he began experimenting with the front dials of the gas burners one night when he crawled out of bed after Ben was asleep. The dishcloth covering my homemade yogurt that was staying warm on the back burner caught fire. (This just happened to be the dial he began experimenting with!) He screamed and ran down toward the basement where Wayne and I were watching TV. Again he knew what to do, and we averted the disaster and calmed him down. Curiosity was huge for Nate; he needed to find out how things worked. We determined to get a childproof stove with dials on top of the stove. (I don't think they even make them that way anymore!) But before we could replace it, he began determinedly warning his brother not to touch the dials with the words "Hot! Hot!" (This was his first word, by the way, even before the words *Mama* or *Dada*.)

So one day, our two boys were in the backyard in a huge sandbox filled with sand with two older playmates from the fourplex. Suddenly, I see Ben, running at full speed and laughing hysterically down the narrow sidewalk between the two apartment buildings. He is running right by our dining room window and straight toward Nicollet Avenue—cars coming both ways! Nathaniel is right behind him, shouting, "Stop! Stop!" This was causing Ben to run all the faster, thinking it was a game, and giggling all the louder!

In a split second, I realized that I could never make it out the front, down the steps, and through the locked entryway to stop him! His precious life and all the multiple miracles flood my mind. A million questions barrage me: Will they both be hit? How am I worthy of these children? Who left the gate open? *Lord, we need a miracle!*

By the time I made it out the door, down the steps, and through the locked apartment entrance door, I saw Nate with his arms clasped tightly around Ben's legs in a wrestling mode, sobbing. I ran across the yard, and we all sat there for what seemed like half an hour (but it was probably only a few minutes), laughing and crying and hugging. I don't think Ben ever realized what had just happened until a few years later, but Nate and I were shaking, crying, and then laughing along with Ben, with our own tears of relief.

I would often remind both boys of how fast and strong Nate was that day. He, with God's help, had saved his brother's life! Whenever the boys have difficulties, I remind them of how much Nate loved Ben to save his life that day! Someone had accidently unlatched the gate, so it was a lesson for all of us. Yet we all know that things happen, we cannot protect our kids all the time, and there are so many things beyond our control. It was good to know that we are ultimately in His hands, with our own guardian angels and His extra power and strength and watch-care over us. It helped me to remember to pray for protection every day for my children.

The second close call happened to Nate on Park Avenue, the one way, four-lane avenue where we had raced to the emergency room with Ben. This was near the time of the first close call, and although Nate was smart, he was not invincible. I believe we had stopped for a garage sale and parked the car. My big, strong husband, Wayne, grabbed Ben and put him on his shoulders, and Nate grabbed my hand and we raced to keep up. Suddenly, Nate dropped my hand and ran back, shouting that he had forgotten his jacket in the car. Before we could stop him, he had dashed into the street, thinking he had seen our car across the street. There was one over there that looked a lot like ours, but it wasn't! As we glanced halfway down the block, four lanes of cars were lined up, and the light was turning green.

Wayne and I both shouted, "Nate, stop! That's not our car!"

Then out of nowhere, it seemed, a large, muscular black man on a bicycle crossed over two lanes to bring him back to the curb just ahead of us. We both ran up, Wayne putting Ben down and shouted thank-yous and hugging and grabbing Nate. When we looked up, the man and bike were gone! We looked up and down the avenue and down both alleyways. No sign of him! His bike just could not move that fast.

We looked to find anyone who had seen what happened. The cars were now whizzing past, and no one was looking back. We believe it to be an angel to this day!

CHAPTER 3

How I Learned What Not To Do

Much of this account is about how God miraculously protected, healed, and saved me and especially my children from unexpected and dangerous circumstances.

I debated in my mind whether to write these two accounts for a long time. For a lot of my life up to this time, God would warn me in different ways that there would be changes ahead. Then when an unexpected change presented itself, I would be prepared for it. Sometimes I would make a mistake and catch myself, and the same mistake, in a more serious context, would present itself a short time later. I would recognize it and avoid some serious consequences. I believe this was God's way of saving me from serious circumstances if I was paying close attention. You know what I mean, learning from one's mistakes. But sometimes He does not save us, especially if we ignore the warning, so that we pay attention and keep the lines of communication open even when life gets very hectic and perhaps overwhelming. It is at these times that it is even more important to spend that time with the Lord and pay attention to that "still, small voice."

Such was the case for this inexperienced, and sometimes not very cautious, young mother of two young boys in the space of fifteen months. God gave me two warnings and yet protected my boys in spite of me.

Car seats and strollers with more than one child can be slow and cumbersome. It will make a simple task like running to the store to pick up a loaf of bread or a gallon of milk into an arduous procedure that will take an hour or more. This was exactly the case for me on two occasions. The first was when I left my nine-month-old son, Ben, at a friend's house, and I took the oldest, Nate, to the doctor for his two-year check-up. On the way home, I realized we were out of milk. He wanted to stay in the car, and *I thought, It will only take five minutes, and I will be right back.*

"Stay in your seat 'til I get back," I told Nate.

"Okay," he replied.

Five minutes later, I was out of Kroger's door. My car was the second car in the very first aisle. So imagine my shock and horror when I saw there was no car! I looked all around the fairly vacant parking lot of about five or so cars, and did not see *my* car!

My thoughts and emotions were running wild: *Did I lock the doors? Yes! He was kidnapped; the car was stolen! Oh my God! I should never have left him! Is anyone around? Are there any witnesses?*

I was ready to scream when I saw it way down at the other side of the parking lot, close up against a light pole… *my car!*

I ran with all my might out there with my heart in my throat.

"Nate, Nate, are you alright?" He was in the driver's seat, crying uncontrollably.

"Yes, yes," he sobs, "I'm sorry, I'm sorry."

Between hugs and sobs of relief on both sides, I finally put together that he had gotten out of his car seat and climbed into the driver's seat, probably knocking the gear-shift out of park to neutral, where it was then. The slight incline of the parking space had caused the car to slowly roll backward, and Nate somehow knew to steer the car back into the aisle, missing the other cars. Then to poor Nate's horror, the car began to very slowly roll forward, and he had steered it all the way across the parking lot, managing to avoid all the cars along the way toward the light pole. He had managed to miss this by inches, with a slight scratch on the side of the car before it finally came to a stop. The incline was hardly perceptible. That was the moment I had ran up beside him. (God's warning: a lot can happen in five minutes!) All I could say was that I was the one who was sorry and that he did a great, great job of steering the car in both directions! No one had seen him, and we just sat there and hugged for five minutes, thanking God.

"He guided you, Nate. It could have been so much worse!" It was a good lesson for both of us.

You would have thought I had learned my lesson on this one, but no. God had to reinforce the lesson before granting me any more children! A few weeks later, Nathaniel, Ben, and I were returning from a fun day at one of the lakes in Minneapolis. Running by a convenience store on the way home, Ben fell fast asleep in his car seat, as it was quite a while past his naptime. He was nine months old (and remember, he took two good naps a day, while Nate now took one). So I decided to walk in with two-year-old Nate in tow, grab a loaf of bread, pay, and return. In my mind, I rationalized, *The car is locked. He can't get out of the bucket seat. I don't want to wake him and get the stroller out.* I did get a check in my spirit, which I brushed aside. So Nathaniel and I went, got the bread, and got in line. But what I didn't count on was a little old man in front of me taking five minutes to get out his change and painstakingly count out a gazillion pennies.

Oh *no*, maybe we should just go. I glanced out the window but couldn't see the area where my car was.

He was nearly done, and I didn't want him to feel bad, so I waited. Finally, I paid, and we walked hand in hand out the door, where we noticed a commotion outside and a police officer. Slowly, we made our way to the car, which was the place of all the commotion. With a look of surprise and dismay, the few people and the officer saw us. With a sigh of relief and maybe a little understanding, they stepped away from the car, where Ben was awake and crying at all the staring people. The policeman, seeing it as his duty, chides me for leaving the child in the car, and I opened the door and hugged and comforted Ben. Then I promised to the officer, the people, and myself that I will *never* do it again.

"That's what they *all* say," he answered.

For whatever reason, he decided not to give me a citation. We sat for a good ten minutes after the hubbub was over, hugging and comforting Ben, being given another lesson and warning, and remembering the still, small, check in my spirit that I did not heed. Seeing the trauma that little Ben went through and my own fear that I could have been reported to Child and Family Services, I felt so stupid! Look what you risked!

Such was the "mediocre mom in a mundane world."

Thank You, God, for Your great mercy and for rescuing us.

This was one of the reasons I would later finish my social work degree in family life education and later work as a counselor in Parents Anonymous and with the Children's Home and Aid Society in Illinois. God *may* rescue us, even when we don't always listen, but He may not!

These are some of the physical ways God can and does protect our children. However, there are many emotional, social, psychological, and spiritual traumas that we cannot foresee or prevent. Or even ones that we, as parents, caused either inadvertently or perhaps knowingly, yet our Heavenly Father wants to heal them all. He is fully able to do that, as He has done for me in many of those areas, and is still doing so. We are all a work in progress.

What we *can* do is to teach our children how the Lord *can* do that and that He *will* do that, if we let Him, and ask Him into those areas where no one else can see. As parents, we need to *ask* for forgiveness for those we are responsible for and to keep the slate clean. We need to be daily examples in front of our children with each other and as husband and wife. This is far easier said than done, but it is a daily task, and the way to teach this is to mentor it and be as transparent as we can. There are healing ministries and Christian counselors and pastors to be found in every denomination.

Childrens' Home and Aid Society of Illinois

CHAPTER 4

God's Healing and Protection

Two years after Ben was born, I had my third child, a boy named David Joseph. I now have three boys in four years. His entrance into our lives brought about a special healing of some of the trauma and fear associated with Ben's birth and meningitis. God is so faithful to bring us through similar circumstances for the purpose of reminding us of His past faithfulness and healing us of fear and doubt.

David was three weeks overdue and weighed almost exactly ten pounds! We can never predict His timing. Nate was born on his due date, Ben was nearly two weeks early, and now David was going on three weeks late! Doctors were concerned I might need to be induced, and I did not want that. For a couple of days, I experienced Braxton-Hicks contractions, and finally, the real labor started. We called our doctor and headed for the hospital. I was apprehensive, remembering the experience with Ben, and yes, we traveled down the same one-way, four-lane street to the same emergency room and hospital.

It was a hot August day, and I was glad to be finally ending this pregnancy in an air-conditioned hospital, but the familiarity of it all was a little bit eerie, if you know what I mean. Prayers from many were with us, and the pregnancy had been normal, except for the three weeks of waiting. The labor went well, and even a little faster than expected. The birth went fine. He was longer and heavier than my previous babies, but no problems. As they wheeled me to my room, I was heaving a great sigh of relief with Wayne at my side.

As I entered the room, I gasped and turned to look at Wayne. In this large hospital, can you imagine my feelings at being placed in the same room, in the same bed by the window, as I was when I had Ben? Wayne double-checked for me that it was the same room number, but I already realized it was the same by its position in the hall with the nurses' station. I must admit it sent shivers up my spine as I looked toward the same bathroom, where I had delivered a blood clot the size of a second baby after being brought to this room with Benjamin. I asked Wayne to pray over this amazing coincidence. They brought David to me, and we had supper together, and all went well. Wayne went home that night, and the next morning, except for a few interruptions for feedings, I slept well. Mother and baby were well, so my doctor released us by evening the next day. This was not before I explained the coincidence to him; however, and he expressed his amazement and congratulations that all had gone well this time.

Both of us remarked, as we drove home that night, that this was no coincidence, but our dear Lord wanted me to relive, remember, and realize His miracle protecting both Ben and I and using His new addition to the family, David, to heal those memories! Thank you, Lord, and thank you, David.

My new life with three boys was now, as you can imagine, hectic, loud, busy, and constant. My husband's late hours and near exhaustion when he would return home, sometimes after the boys' bedtime, could leave us unable to have time or ability to really communicate what was going on in our separate lives. We were busy with meetings (men's and women's small groups, midweek meetings, school, and preschool performances and activities). You just have to be young and energetic to keep up with the life and schedule of three small children. With me being a stay-at-home mom, I pretty much had to wait until Wayne was home to go out to the store, get a babysitter for a doctor's appointment for one of them, or go out in the evening at all.

I was beginning to resent my choice to have children and our timing, with two in diapers and one potty training. How do moms do it? A working mom's life was beginning to look very attractive. We did not have anyone over very often; the house was always a mess, and it was just too much work! My parents and Wayne's were hundreds of miles away in opposite directions and not able to help us with the children in any way, let alone my emotional and mental exasperation. A couple of times, during a depressing moment, I would actually entertain thoughts of suicide.

One night, after a burglar had broken into our house and the police came, and I was feeling as upset about how terrible the house looked as I was about the break-in, I lay in bed just shaking. (Police did catch him by the way!) I was feeling so not up to this job as a mother in this big and dangerous city. We had left our inside back door open, while all the other tenants had locked theirs. Then a while later, I had a real nightmare. I was standing at that same back door at the end of our long hall, and a small dog was nosing open the door and whining. I went to investigate, only to find a huge lion ready to pounce on the door. I quickly began trying to get the door closed with all my might and was not succeeding! The lion let out a huge roar, and I screamed for Wayne. He came up quickly behind me, and together we closed and bolted the door.

It was so vivid. I found myself waking my husband and tearfully telling him about the frightening dream, thinking it must mean something. He listened carefully and thought for a while. This was unusual because Wayne was a deep sleeper, and I thought he would just turn over and go back to sleep, but he, too, thought there was a meaning. Then he said he thought he had the interpretation.

He said God showed him that the lion was a spirit of anger in my life and the dog was self-pity. They were both trying to destroy me, even kill me! Then for the first time, I shared with him my feelings of despair and even of suicide. We agreed in prayer to cast out these destroying demons. Over the next few weeks and months, I would identify these feelings and come against them with Wayne's help and realize they were not really me. After that dream and interpretation, I never really felt those suicidal feelings again or the anger and self-pity as my own. I was set free, yet with a clear picture of the danger of entertaining those feelings in my heart and life, and especially where they came from. I have shared this story with many over the years to help others get free of emotional snares in their lives.

After a few months, we had moved to a new house in Minneapolis. This was on another busy street, Chicago Avenue. For those familiar with the city, we were one block from Lake Street, where the recent devastation occurred for blocks after the death of George Floyd. This was over forty years ago and only a few blocks from the intersection of his death. It was a rough and scary neighborhood back then, with squad cars ending up on both houses on either side of us the first month after moving in. One was for an abusive tenant; the other was drug related. God's protection was evident over our children, our church (one block back through the alley), and an Ethiopian immigrant, fleeing for his life from his native country, as we housed him and fed him until he was transferred to an air force job in Oklahoma. We were able to help several hurting people while living there.

No, the miraculous protection I remember in this house came not from dangerous people or this neighborhood but from a tornado, or straight-line winds as it was called. We had just purchased a beautiful dining room table and chairs and were rushing home. A storm was brewing, and we needed to get it home and moved in before the wind and rain came. We rushed the boys inside and moved the table up the stairs and into the house. We had just gotten inside and let out a breath from exhaustion when we heard the loud sound of a freight train just behind us. In this area of Minnesota, tornados are rare, but I grew up in Illinois, and the sound of a tornado siren was at least a yearly event, and we had seen the damage close by many a time. In Chicago, my grandmother lost her house to a tornado as a child, so we took this sound very seriously.

"To the basement, everyone!" we shouted, but after two steps toward the door while still in the living room, we heard a tremendous crash. Crouching for cover, we realized we were all too late. All was suddenly quiet, so we peeked out the front window to see the huge hundred-year-old tree in our front yard split in half, with the left half just missing our car and the car next door, extending out into the street. If it had fallen toward the house, we would have been directly in its path; all of us at the front window!

We later found out that it was indeed a tornado that had torn down every tree on the entire block, one block over just west of us. Some roofs were damaged; one house was severely hit. To this day, that one block has only small saplings instead of the mature trees like ours to the north and to the south. Our old oak tree was the only one hit on our block, yet it damaged no cars or houses. Tornadoes are rare in Minneapolis, yet God's protection was on our little family!

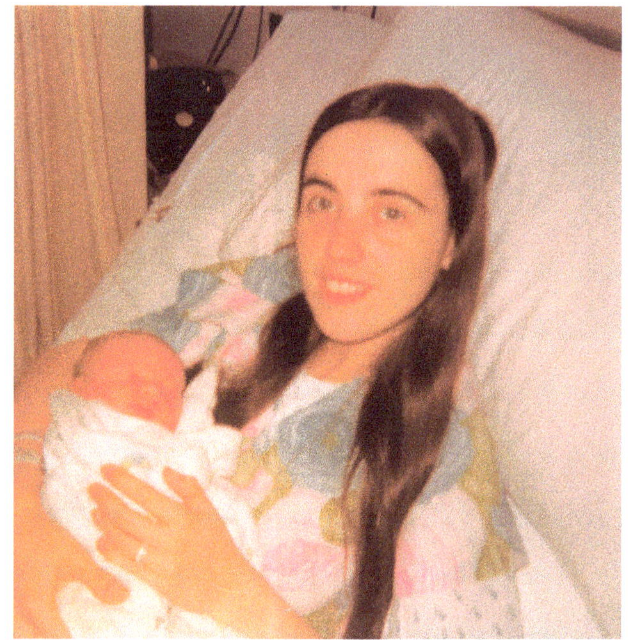

Nate day 1

Ben day 3

Nate, Ben, and Dave

Wayne holding son

CHAPTER 5

Rock Climbing at Taylor Falls, Fears, and Encounters

"Do you really want to climb that big old rocky cliff, Nate?" I asked, pensively.

"Yah! C'mon, Dad, can we?"

Wayne looked at the fifteen-foot craggy rock wall on the side of our path, wandering through the beautiful park along the river at Taylor Falls State Park, Minnesota. He studied the height and footholds with little Ben in the sturdy backpack carrier on his shoulders, and then said,

"Yaya, I think we can do it!"

I looked at Ben's reaction, and he was all excited, so I kept my mouth shut concerning the suggestion to leave us behind and let them climb it. So quickly, Nate goes up, Dad goes behind, and I follow in the rear (trying to follow in Wayne's footsteps, although his stride is twice my own). I was a bit slower than them, and suddenly, all three of them were on top, running around to clamber down the grassy incline.

"Wait, wait!"

"*Oh*, Mom, you can do it!"

As I looked around and down to where they were laughing and talking underneath me, I froze! They have no idea how petrified I feel, and my memory as a teenager in the Rocky Mountains with my fellow students at Bear Trap Ranch comes flooding back. We had spent the morning hiking just beside Pike's Peak, and had "conquered," or reached the peak of a smaller nearby mountain. As we descended, our leader thought some of us might want to try rappelling from the facing cliff. I was actually thinking it would be fun as he explained the process and the safety ropes. I watched the first volunteer, but when I glanced over the cliff, I was suddenly not so sure. I wish I had had the guts, and I would not have been so frightened of this little cliff, but now my hands were becoming extremely sweaty.

"C'mon, Mom, hurry up. You can do it! There are two places for your hand and foot!"

He was right; it was only a few more hand and foot holds to the top. Yet my hands were still sweaty. It seemed like twenty minutes, me hesitating there, but it was only a few minutes. I saw myself in my mind's eye falling to my death right in front of my two boys and Wayne. That was enough to grab sanity and pray desperately: *Lord, calm me and help me. I know you don't want me to traumatize my family!*

Miraculously, I felt His presence, and the panic and perspiration were gone! I quickly made the last three hand and footholds and clambered down the side and back to my family. My heart still beating and pounding in my chest, we continued down the path and had a wonderful day. I told Wayne about it later. I truly believe God can deliver us from irrational fears and give moms the power to overcome!

Wayne has had deliverance from an irrational fear of the dark and the road ending ahead of us when we were in college, and I had a simple prayer answered concerning bad dreams as a nine-year-old child. These are good stories to relate to your children at appointed times to help them understand how we were vulnerable and scared once too. They will relate and open up when we share our present and past weaknesses and how God helps in those hard times. This is the time to cast out a spirit of fear and recognize where it is coming from, for "God does not give us a spirit of fear but of love and of a sound mind" (2 Timothy 1:7 KJV).

David was just over a year old when we moved to Michigan and bought our first home. Interest rates were double digits in the late '70s and the first opportunity for us to buy was not in Minnesota but in Ypsilanti, Michigan. We were able to find a cute three-bed, two-bath home in a nice neighborhood at 5 percent interest for three years, then it would balloon to the going rate. Well, we could afford that payment and were so happy to move into a more "normal" setting for our growing family. Little did we know that we were in for a new set of perplexing problems.

Nice neighbors and, yes, even more importantly, Christian families struggle with their kids and sexual messages. Moms and dads need to be careful of naiveté. We need to be keeping up with what is going on in schools and with your children's friends. Things have changed drastically, and parents need to keep up with the details of what friends are saying and what school and even church folks are telling our kids. We, as parents, have a constitutional and religious right to raise our children according to our beliefs.

Our three boys—aged two, four, and five—now all have new struggles to deal with. In the next few years in this "nice" neighborhood, they would have to deal with bullies, babysitters, porn, and even perversion in a nearby park. At school, a neighborhood third-grade girl would stalk and beat up our first-grade son until he secretly found a different way home. A male "babysitter" preyed upon our unwilling son. We were so blessed to have Nate tell us immediately, and we were able to discuss it with the parents and the boy, who was extremely embarrassed. He finally admitted it, and it was a learning experience for both of our families. Neighborhood "church-going" families' children managed to get their hands on very indecent material and pass it around to our children. These confrontations are difficult and painful, but always worth it in the long run. I encourage all concerned parents to make the effort and not ignore the warning signs. It is how children can discern, at an early age, right from wrong. I especially encourage you, as parents, to sit down and talk about why, from a scriptural point of view, these things are wrong.

Make time for this and never put it off, even if life gets in the way; we did not always do this and would live to regret it as the years passed. Honest communication forewarned us many times, and being that the three of them stuck together a lot, it helped tremendously. Yet there are many things I probably did not hear about. Here is where trust in God and listening prayer are a must. Guard your heart. Areas of sin that parents are weak in will inevitably plague their children. God can, and has, and always will, heal and forgive us (Oswald Chambers, *My Utmost for His Highest*, March 30–31).

Being good role models, not hypocrites, admitting fault and receiving forgiveness and healing, guarding and blessing our children while we still can, is God's best. My naiveté blinded me to some changes in the accepted norm of the day and real dangers that were not at all part of my own growing up years. Please be aware of becoming too busy with school (your own or theirs), house, or job to see what is happening right before your eyes, in your neighborhood, and with your best friends.

Wisdom, kindness, understanding, honesty, and the freedom for them to talk, and for you to listen, are so important. We all start out poorly, but we can get better and better at this! Now in this age of lack of innocence down to the kindergarten level for such things as sex education, including transgender issues, explicit books in our school libraries, and teaching on critical race theory, we have some very important decisions to make. Are we going to monitor the public school system as involved parents, put our children in a private school where we can agree and trust, or consider home schooling, as we did forty years ago? All these avenues are very important and needed in our current day and age. It is more important than ever to be able to talk frankly and biblically with our children. You need to ask, "Do you and your children read and move toward understanding the *entire* Bible?" There is so much to discuss, interpret, and apply in that book. Sometimes, Wayne and I would discuss everything we, as adults, had questions about but often failed to include our children in pertinent discussions. None of us know it all, and every viewpoint is important to be heard and considered.

CHAPTER 6

Homebirth: Our First Girl!

Four years have now gone by. We had been growing more confident as parents. Yes, momma wanted a little girl. I had hoped that my third child might be a girl, but three boys and a girl seemed to be the pattern in Wayne's family. David was a ten-pound, strapping baby boy, so now I thought it was time. I had two good friends with large families who had decided to become midwives. This was becoming a growing trend. Many parents were learning how to use minimal pain medications, have Lamaze births using breathing techniques, nursing their babies, and some have their babies at home. I had been successful with the first four and was willing to trust my friends for the home birth.

All was going well, and my checkups were good. I believe it was not possible to know the sex of your child before birth at this time, but I was not gaining as much weight and was really hoping for a girl this time. My midwife friend was out of town for my monthly check, but she recommended another doctor. I called this doctor, who was out of town also, but she recommended a third. I made the appointment.

When it became time, I went in and had my examination. He seemed a little brusque. I began to feel uneasy, uncomfortable, and a bit hurried and abrupt. Did I detect some dismissiveness in my questions? I was close to five months pregnant and began to feel this was a mistake. I seriously did not like his attitude and, in some ways, felt "dirty" as he touched me and wanted out of there!

As I was getting dressed, he called (rather than asked) me into his office. I made sure to leave the door open. When I had seated myself, he asked me how many children I had. This was really getting strange. I told him, and he looked straight at me and said, "You have a good family. You don't need any more."

"What do you mean? I am pregnant!" I replied. (Did he talk like this to all his patients?)

"Do you really want this child? You can do something about this, you know."

Suddenly, I got his drift and began moving toward the door. "Yes, I do!"

How could I have been referred to such a doctor as this! I half ran and walked past the receptionist and out the door. As I passed the nurse, I heard her saying to someone on the phone, "Don't worry, there is often a lot of bleeding after a procedure like yours."

I was in an abortion doctor's office! I was so mad, I was trembling and had to slow down my speeding car and calm myself. Then I began to sob as I realized what they were trying to do. If I was a vulnerable young unmarried girl, I could have considered his proposal and given in to his bullish coercion. Later, I wish that I had stayed and given him a piece of my mind for his attitude, but at the time, I was just in shock.

A couple of years later, I would find myself in front of this office, sitting on the floor and being carried out by policemen (who were very understanding, by the way, and some were supportive) involved in a project called Operation Rescue. We were passively protesting abortion clinics by lying limp in front of them, preventing their operation until we were carried away by the police. We did community service as a punishment, and that was a pleasure!

Back to my daughter, who was born at home with my midwives a few months later. She was a healthy baby girl, a little over eight pounds. My mom was staying with us from Illinois. She was such a beautiful baby and my first girl, so I was the happiest mom in the world! She was born at eight o'clock in the morning on the twenty-eighth of June, and so at that time of the day, everyone was up, including my three boys. They ran out the door shouting, "My mom just had a baby! It's a girl!" up and down the block. Some of the neighbors knew she was born at home. If they did not, the boys told them! Her name was Talitha (Aramaic for *little lamb*) Joy. I had a sweet baby shower with all new baby girl clothes, and I could get out dolls and tea sets and flowers all over her room.

I remember about a month before I became very emotional when I found a mother robin from our backyard, dead from a neighborhood boy's BB gun on our sidewalk and heard the baby birds chirping desperately for hours before they died. I became teary-eyed for the next two days, really an overreaction but was it an unconscious response to the reality of what was going on in that abortion clinic in Ann Arbor? I do not know, but I know that I was overjoyed and relieved at the birth of my daughter, my little lamb, that was not led to the slaughter.

I had been against abortion during the '70s and was preparing to debate the issue in my senior year in high school and first two years in college, when suddenly, the issue was moot when the Supreme Court ruled in *Roe v. Wade*. Wow, the majority of Americans did not rule in this case.

Yet this was more of an intellectual response. After having four children of my own, I became even more pro-life. I wanted to help expectant mothers in any way I could, helping them to decide to keep their babies. Wayne also strongly believed as I did. We began to find out that most people in this decade had not thought very much about this issue, including both sets of our parents, unless they were directly involved with someone making that decision. If I had not gone through this experience with the referral doctor, I may never have gotten involved either. More and more, I was realizing how much the Bible had to say about knowing us even before we were conceived in our mother's womb (Jeremiah 1:5 NIV). We became involved in the politics of the issue, then with pregnancy counseling centers and homes for unwed mothers.

Still it didn't seem we were changing many people's minds and had no idea this issue would grow and grow in the coming years. When we heard about Randall Terry and his passive resistance movement called Operation Rescue and a chapter was being organized in the Ypsilanti/Ann

Arbor area, we wanted to get involved immediately. Wayne traveled to New York with support from area Christian ministries, including Dave Wilkerson. With this decision came his first arrest and release. This became the pattern all over the country. We rescued in Ann Arbor and Ypsilanti persistently until the clinic in Ypsilanti was closed, and I believe there has never been another one since. We rescued in Atlanta, Georgia, with Randall Terry until he was jailed for an extended time, and eventually, our passive protest became outlawed all over the country with the application of a criminal law against "racketeering" which was intended for mobsters.

So the birth of our precious daughter started a whole new chapter in our lives. I was able to share her with many mothers as the beautiful girl that an abortion doctor tried to talk me into aborting because our family was getting "too large and expensive." God has blessed us tremendously with Talitha Joy, and we now have two beautiful grand-daughters! We went on to have one more dear son, Andrew Jonathon.

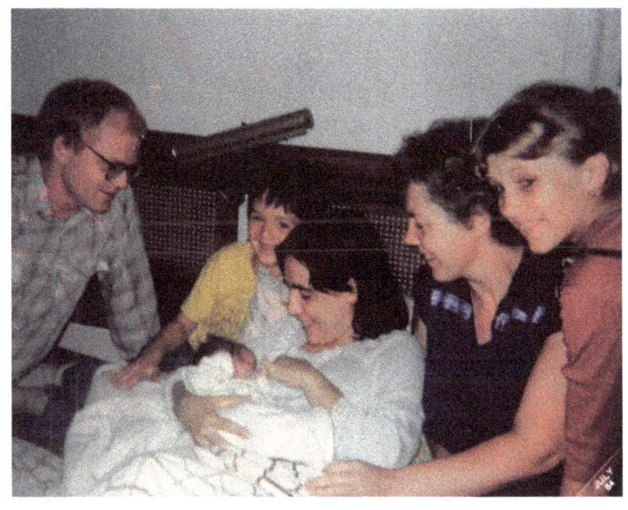

CHAPTER 7

Another Dramatic Angel Story

Four years after Talitha was born, we had another ten-pound baby boy named Andrew Jonathon. We ended up calling him by his middle name, Jon or Jonathon. He was a bit of a disappointment to our four-year-old daughter, who so much wanted a baby sister, but he became a dear favorite of his three brothers. His temperament was more like Ben's, a gentle, quiet spirit. We had only three bedrooms in this big farmhouse, and so Talitha had a bedroom all to herself. That left our youngest sharing a bedroom with his three brothers, so they became very close. Often, he would fall asleep on the sofa, and we would just cover him with a blanket and let him sleep. He later shared with us that he felt that he never really had his own space. He was so easygoing that we never thought as much about it as we did our eldest, who at his age was a little more vocal about his desires. (We wish we had been a little more sensitive to Jon's quieter spirit.) We did later create a bedroom on the main floor for Nate. When the boys were off to college, Jon and Talitha each had their own room when he was in third grade.

We had moved out to the country and had nearly two acres of lawn and trees with a treehouse and a fort for the boys to roam about in. We had decided to homeschool along with my two midwives and several other families in the Ypsilanti area. We had a huge, horse barn and a garage with a loft. Jon was a curious tagalong for the other big boys and his sister and their friends. So one day, Wayne had the stairway to the loft down, and the boys, Talitha, and a friend were having a "club" meeting. Unbeknownst to us, they decided to have a meeting up there. Wayne was working around the garage, and Jon was outside too. Well, he heard what was going on in the loft, and curiosity led him up the steps to see what it was all about. He was about six and a half at the time, and when he got to the top, he began to stand and walk over to the corner where they were planning things. As he approached, the neighbor girl gave him a "What are *you* doing here?" kind of look, and he began backing up.

Yes, you guessed it; he overstepped backward, and before his siblings could stop him, he went tumbling down the ladder. Wayne had just stepped into the room from outside, and, quick as he was to respond, he did not make it to the cement floor under the last step to break his fall. Right before his eyes, he saw Jonathon's head hit the cement, but there was no crack. In fact, there was not even a sound. This was a fall from about eight feet, and he ended up with no injuries!

He later complained about an achy shoulder, but Wayne witnessed it firsthand and said there was no way he could make that fall and not have at least a bump on his head, or more like a fractured skull! It was almost like someone invisible had pillowed his head and cushioned his fall.

Again, his guardian angel? I did not hear the complete details of this event until a few years later! They all told me that they hid these events from me because they did not want to upset or worry me, but they each experienced the awe that their father did, especially Jon himself! They felt it was a miracle that he ended up with not even a bruise!

That was only one of the amazing things that happened with Jon. We had another storm where lightning struck a very old and tall tree next to the house. Talitha had run to the basement, but no tornado siren had sounded, and the crack from the strike had already been heard. As we were peering out the window, Jon told us that he was seeing angel wings rising and falling at the corners of the house through the large windows. We stared but saw nothing. Later after the storm, one of my midwives, who lived down the road, told me she was driving by the house just before the storm and distinctly saw angels on each corner of our house and knew we were being protected. We found the huge branch from the tree and the burned wood down the trunk, but again, it missed our house and two cars completely.

Sometimes children are much more sensitive to the spiritual world than hardened adults. David, our third, also talked of seeing the face of Jesus on the open inside wall of our church during a service about His care and tenderness.

Jon loved his brothers dearly and would refer to them as the brothers in plural. He had a tender heart and, as they were entering adolescence and high school, he would tearfully warn them not to smoke or get into other bad habits. He was often more effective than us as parents. He was one of my quickest learners for homeschooling and often learned a lot from my reading instruction for his big sister. We did a program called Sing, Spell, Read, and Write, and he was advancing not far behind her, teaching himself to read with the songs. I later used a number of these songs in my eight years of kindergarten teaching. Songs are such a fun way to learn!

As two of our sons went off to college—Nate to Minneapolis College of Art and Design and Ben to Michigan State University—he began to feel the loss of his lifelong companions. The brothers were now splitting apart. I only had two homeschooled students at home at that time since David was entering high school. I was working part-time at a small rural library and taking night classes to finish my degree in family life education. My mother in Illinois began having some serious issues with mental and physical health, and I wanted to be there for her. We were able to sell our house and land and to buy a smaller house in a town not far from my parents' home. It was the first time we would own our home outright with no mortgage! We also found a very good school system with values we could agree with.

So began another major move from Ypsilanti, Michigan, to Chatsworth, Illinois. I was ready to get involved in a job and a career, and my two children were going to attend public school for the first time. There were lots of changes, but I did not recognize a major problem. David, our third son, was now entering his senior year, and

I had been so involved in teaching, the library, and finishing my degree that I did not see how hard this was for him. He came to visit the high school but just could not stomach the thought of leaving his friends and attending his last year in a sea of strangers. He found a good friend whose family would adopt him for this last year, and he insisted on staying in Ypsilanti. This came as a shock after we had signed on the house in Illinois. I have to admit, this was an area of failed communication on my part, very understandable on his part, and largely overlooked by me and perhaps Wayne too.

I had a hard time that first year in Illinois, and so did Jon, and later we realized Talitha, too, would have some difficult adjustments. The brothers were all gone now for Jon, and we had a hard time deciding where to place him in school. Talitha was entering junior high, and it would be very hard socially for him to be home alone and home-schooled when he was so quick to learn. We decided to have him take third grade because that was the grade level for his age. It was very easy for him, boring, but his teacher was a gem, and we still know her to this day. She was aware of his numerous adjustment problems and took extra care and understanding of his anger at missing his brothers and making adjustments to school and new, very different friends. He continued to excel academically and learned to cope very well in middle school.

The last incident that I want to share about Jonathon happened in middle school with a bully/friend who, at one point, smashed and left his bike and laughed about it. Jon went to him and forgave him and did not let it cause a rift between them. I was amazed and told him that I didn't know if I could have done the same thing, especially at the age he was. To this day, the boys, now men, have remained friends, and his mother and I are friends. There is great admiration for my son. He simply responds that he felt God told him to do it. I do believe it had an impact on that boy's life.

Well, there are many more stories I could tell about these boys' lives, but these are some of the ones that stand out for me. Now I want to talk more about my daughter. God has been faithful in protecting our family over and over. Sometimes we must make serious decisions that may not always be popular for all of us in a large family. David stayed in Ypsilanti and went on to marry a woman from Ann Arbor. She is an exceptional teacher and a wonderful, godly mother, and we have two beautiful granddaughters, ages eight and fourteen. If he had not courageously decided to finish his senior year there, he may never have met Jenn. At some point, we must let go, and this was probably the hardest point of my life, but my new career in social work came to occupy a lot of my time. Jon and the brothers are still very close to this day and work hard to get the whole family together at least once every other year!

Dave and Jon at basketball

David, a *Star Wars* geek

Dave in Music Man

Nate, Jon, Dave, Ben

"We thought you might need the evidence to prove it."

Celebrate Dave's long-awaited graduation with us on:
Saturday, June 18th.

Festivities will begin at 2pm at our home:

3190 Braeburn Circle
Ann Arbor, MJ 48108
975-1848

We hope to see you there!

CHAPTER 8

A Daughter is More Important Than a Paid-For House

As I contemplate writing my last chapter, I hope to share a decision we made that we will never regret. Maybe we learned something about keeping communication lines open with our children since our last move. I sure hope so. We were down to only two children now, yet I have a full-time job and both children were in public school. Talitha, up to this time, has had a nice assortment of friends at church, homeschool, and neighbors. She seems to be a social butterfly and finds it naturally easy to make friends and influence them in a positive way.

In our little town of Chatsworth, a bedroom community as Wayne liked to put it, we were experiencing small-town living for the first time in our lives. We had both grown up in larger or suburban areas. Everyone knows everyone, or if they don't, they automatically wave as you drive by, thinking they must! So we wave back. Talitha lost no time in meeting three friends riding on the bus from the next town where the junior high was located. Only the elementary school was in Chatsworth, one park, a bank, and a few shops in a two-block downtown area. The middle school and junior high were in Forrest, a little larger town; and the high school was in the biggest of the three, Fairbury.

As the year progressed, we began to realize how observed and open our lives were to the people all around us, and that, in some ways, Chatsworth was the "tail" and not the "head," if you know what I mean. Talitha began to make other friends who were in different towns and churches and of higher achievement levels. We were happy to see this, but her friends in town began to take it the wrong way. For some reason, she got on their bad side, and they began calling her with annoying messages.

We had a talk about how she might respond to these calls, and she realized that she would not mind losing them as friends because this behavior was not acceptable. So we talked about what to do: hang up, retort in kind (no, that would bring her down to their level), yell (no, that would show them they were getting a rise out of her). We prayed and knew that she would, on her own, know what to do. The next time she got the call, here's what I heard her say:

"Oh, why don't you get a life?" and hung up.

She never got another call!

Thank You, Lord!

Well, these were just some of the things that can happen to a new junior high girl, and I wondered if we had made the right decision to put her in school, but she made some other good friends. I made an effort to take excursions with these friends to places like Champaign and

Bloomington/Normal. They were a fun bunch of girls and began to call themselves the six-pack. Most of them lived on farms or in the larger town of Fairbury. Talitha began to want to spend a lot of time in their town, and as high school was approaching, we began to realize how much time and money we would need to invest in getting her to all her activities. Talitha liked choir, art, and sports. She was a runner like her dad and big brother.

Chatsworth had gotten a reputation for being a poorer and "dirty" town, like the other side of the tracks. I knew what this felt like a little bit in one of the places I had to move to as a child. Whether this was warranted or not (I did not think it was), we found ourselves traveling to Fairbury for a church we liked there and shopping a lot at Dave's, where they actually carried out your groceries! They still do this to this very day!

Well, you guessed it. We began looking for a house in Fairbury, which reminded me a lot of Mayberry on *The Andy Griffith Show*! (If I had time, I would tell you a real Barney Fife story in the police department. Maybe I will write a story about Fairbury.)

We did find a nice house in Fairbury, and Talitha went on to be friends with these five other girls for the rest of her life. The six-pack went on to graduate from high school, all members of the honor society, and they still have reunions every so often. Jon was also in the band and choir. They both became members of the Madrigals, and they did so many other activities, including art shows and sports.

Yes, we had to get another mortgage, but I wonder if they would have enjoyed high school as much or have become the people they are today if we had stayed in that original town and kept our house because it was paid for. I believe God prompted us to move for our daughter's sake, and it turned out to be the best for all of us. In fact, it was in that town that we found two more houses to buy and flip, doubling our buying price. It was in that town that we made good friends with all our neighbors and experienced the very best of small-town living!

Senior Prom

Dad, Ben, Talitha, Mom

CHAPTER 9

Another Experience That Changed My Life!

As I close this book, I am reminded of one last experience that changed the focus of my life completely. Sometimes, if you are obedient to the Lord in a bold, courageous, and difficult way, you may be surprised by a supernatural experience. We have all heard accounts of near-death experiences and maybe even seen some accounts on TV of visions or dreams that the recipients claimed were from God. Well, each one needs to be evaluated on its own merits. But doctors and scientists are telling us that many of these cannot be passed off as mere hallucinations or drug-related side effects.

Well, I did not have a near-death experience (unless my near-falling experience on the rock-climbing expedition could be described as a mild one). Yet I did have an experience like none other, either before or since. We had made a very daring decision to bring our entire family of seven in a small camper from Michigan down to Atlanta, Georgia.

The previously mentioned organization and endeavor called Operation Rescue, headed by Randall Terry, was rescuing indefinitely in Atlanta area abortion clinics.

We sat down in front of a clinic (like a sit-in) before they opened their doors and would not move, thereby delaying the opening until police could come out and pick us up and carry us off to jail. This gave trained counselors an opportunity to talk to clients before they could get inside. They were able to refer to pro-life clinics close by to help with costs, baby clothes, and homes until the child was born, and then assistance, childcare, and job referrals after the baby. So we *do* have a police record, the only record for which we are very proud.

It was a decision that both my husband and I felt very strongly about, but to many, it may seem reckless and without thought for the best interests of our children or careers. We were very aware of this, and yet both of us felt it was acting in obedience to the Lord. We knew it would take a lot of faith to believe He would guide us day by day as to where we should go, how we should live, and how long we should stay. We felt that, finally, we were doing something actively to object to a law we felt was against God's law in a way that was active and not just passively voting. We were even open to the idea that the Lord might want us to relocate there. It was definitely a leap of faith. Again I thought of Abraham being called out of his city and relatives to obey God and go to a land that He would show him.

Whether this predisposed me to this experience, I do not know, but it was certainly an adventure! I certainly no longer saw myself as a mediocre mom in a mundane world of monotony. Yet I do not believe there was anything special about myself or our family to experience something like this without a responsibility to share and write and talk about it, whether anyone believes me or not.

Well, here it goes…

We were sitting in a church in Marietta, Georgia. There were a little over a hundred in attendance, and we were reading aloud the passage in Revelation 19:11–16 (NIV): "I saw heaven standing open, and there before me was a white horse whose rider is called faithful and true. With justice, he judges and makes war. His eyes are like blazing fire, and on his head are many crowns. He has a name written on him that no one knows but himself. He is dressed in a robe dipped in blood, and his name is Word of God. The armies of heaven are following him, riding on white horses and dressed in fine linen white and clean. Out of his mouth comes a sharp sword with which to strike down the nations. 'He will rule them with an iron scepter.' He treads the winepress of the fury of the wrath of God Almighty. On his robe and on his thigh, he has this name written: KING OF KINGS AND LORD OF LORDS." (Please read this familiar passage before moving on.) I have later been told this may have been an "open" vision, although I had never heard of anything like this. As we were reading, I experienced this. I was wide awake and able to see and hear the service before me, but time seemed to have stopped, or I was transcended or above reality, something I had never experienced before. I was lifted high, transported to behold a high, rocky mountain and cliff. Jutting out on the cliff was a white stallion, rearing up, beautiful and terrible. His eyes were wild, red, and angry, almost ferocious, with its mane and tail flying in the wind. With muscles rippling, he was rearing and pawing in the air.

There was no saddle on his back. The rider, who appeared to be as strong and capable as his mount, was none other than the Son of God himself, with a crown declaring faithful and true, as the scripture described. There were details not mentioned—his short, straight hair blowing wildly in the wind like the horse's mane. His eyes were dark and intense, sparkling with fire. As he expertly controlled the rearing stallion—now to the right, now to the left—there were sometimes crowns, a crown, or no crowns. I watched in awe as he struggled to hold back the steed with both hands, taking the short sword in his right hand to his mouth, clutching it in his teeth so as to hold back the stallion with both hands, who wanted to charge ahead. Both had this fire in their eyes, full of determination yet being held back, waiting for a signal it seemed.

I suddenly realized that I was in some kind of hologram, to the best that I could describe it, because I could dart around, seeing them from every angle in full amazement and more than living color. Jesus was dressed in a dazzling white robe with strong hands capable of holding the white mane and soothing and calming the impatient stallion. The robe flowed and whipped around his legs and feet. Yes, his feet were a deep golden bronze, very beautiful, with no scars that I could see. They clung tightly to the horse's flank as the horse reared and turned. The four corners of his robe were brilliantly red and dripping with very fresh blood. I had never seen such bright red blood against such dazzling white linen. It was a startling and almost blinding sight to see. On his belt, crowns, and, I believe, sword were gold inscribed letters *Word of God.* (*Logos* may have been on the sword too.)

On a scarlet sash, crossing from his right shoulder to his left thigh like a banner, were the words *King of kings* and *Lord of lords* embroidered in gold. His feet and ankles were shiny, suntanned bronze, beautiful to behold—the most beautiful feet I had ever seen! This, our king, struck me as totally awesome and terrible at the same time. I find it so hard to find words to describe what I saw and felt as I continued to dart around this figure, like a fairy, and realized that the service was beginning to end with a hymn.

As I watched, some of these articles would appear and then be gone (his sash, the crowns, the sword, the belt).

Finally, as he was continuing to control the stallion who was prancing in every direction, I became aware of His eyes on me (I had actually felt invisible in this "hologram"). These eyes turned from being intense and fiery to the kindest eyes I had ever seen, yet they were still very intense. Without any words, he conveyed the urgency of the moment. What He was waiting for was for His army to be in line behind Him and in perfect order. They needed to be in file and rank, armed and ready before he could let the stallion charge! He was waiting for *us*! I must help Him in warning them to get in order behind Him!

That is when the scene shifted to the mountain below us. There were little clefts and crags and small caves in the rock surrounding and descending in every direction down the mountain. Men, women, and children were huddled in rags, hiding and shivering—some in clusters, some in pairs, and some all alone. I saw myself flying down, shouting to them and pointing up at the King above them.

"Look!" I shouted in urgent excitement. "Look! Just look at *who* is above you!"

As soon as someone responded and looked, astonishment filled their being and illumined them. Instantly, their rags transformed into shining armor, as described in Ephesians 6:10–20 (NIV), the armor of God. They stood tall, with their faces lifted high, and began to turn around, climb up the mountain, and get into rank-and-file position, listening to the gentle orders of the Master. Some never looked, but many were transformed, and the urgency displayed by all of us was tangible. Our King was waiting and holding back until every last transformed soldier was in his place. Then I knew that this lovely, fearsome animal would be released to charge!

I heard the last hymn being sung and an ending prayer from the pastor, and my eyes streaming with tears, I filed out silently with my family, my surroundings all returning to normal. I was so shaken that I could not speak for quite a while, even after we were in the car. Eventually, I shared, to the best of my ability, what I had experienced. I have not shared this experience in its entirety with very many people, but it has brought a new intensity to my personal testimony and desire to share God's love with others, all who will listen.

My friend, are you in place in the King's army? He is waiting for *you*!

> Wake up, sleeper, rise from the dead, and
> Christ will shine on you! (Ephesians 5:14
> NIV)

FINAL CHAPTER

Epilogue

As I close this account, I hope these stories encourage, bring hope, and demonstrate that we all have decisions to make about the *hard* circumstances that come into our lives: physical, emotional, social, spiritual, and financial.

I am just an ordinary person, quite mediocre, with no special talents that anyone around me could see, at least at a young age. The key to life is how we respond to the difficult circumstances that come into our lives. All of us have or will have them, one kind or another! If we are open to God's intervention, He will come into our lives and have a relationship with us, making our lives a marvel to behold. Everyone has this choice no matter who you are: broken, bruised, crushed, or just mediocre like me. Your life can be wonderfully and marvelously full of purpose for eternity.

Today I have given you the CHOICE between LIFE and DEATH, between blessings and curses. I call on heaven and earth to witness the choice you make. Oh, that you would CHOOSE LIFE, that you and your descendants might live! (Deuteronomy 30:19 NLT)

Top—Nate, Dave, Wayne, Ben
Bottom—Carol, Jon, Talitha

About the Author

Carol J. Nelson saw herself as a very ordinary A/B student with a lifelong curiosity about God. She strived and struggled to be really good at something—music, art, science, nursing, math, even religion and philosophy. Finally, she decided to settle for a family. Eventually, she went on to get a degree in social work, became a librarian, and then a Christian school teacher. But her favorite was being a mom of five children, which she discovered to be anything but mundane or mediocre.